CLASSICAL WEDDING FAVORITES

CONTENTS

WITHDRAWN

ISBN 0-634-02585-6

HAL•LEONARD®
CORPORATION

7777 W. BLUEMOUND RD. P.O. BOX 13819 MILWAUKEE, WI 53213

Visit Hal Leonard Online at
www.halleonard.com

AIR ON THE G STRING
from ORCHESTRAL SUITE NO. 3

By JOHANN SEBASTIAN BACH

Slowly and stately

ALLEGRO MAESTOSO
from WATER MUSIC

By GEORGE FRIDERIC HANDEL

Allegro maestoso

AVE MARIA

By FRANZ SCHUBERT

AVE MARIA
based on Prelude in C Major by J.S. Bach

By CHARLES GOUNOD

Moderately, with motion

With pedal

BE THOU WITH ME
(Bist du bei mir)

By JOHANN SEBASTIAN BACH

BRIDAL CHORUS
from LOHENGRIN

By RICHARD WAGNER

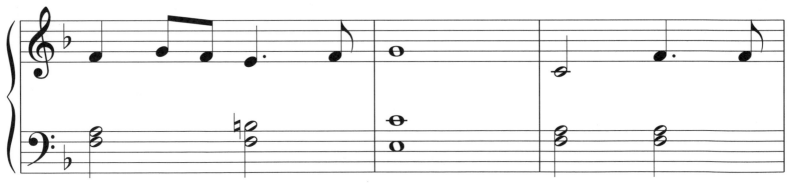

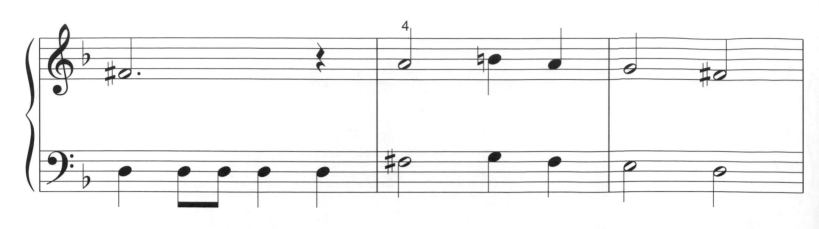

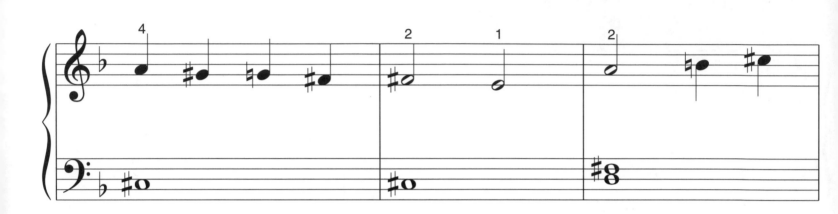

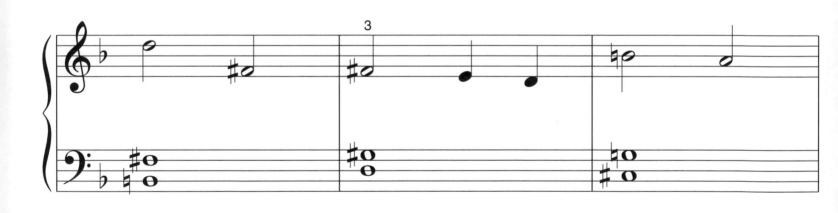

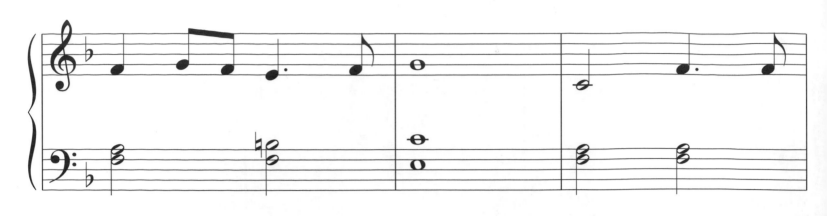

CANON IN D MAJOR

By JOHANN PACHELBEL

ENTREAT ME NOT TO LEAVE THEE

(Song of Ruth)

Words and Music by
CHARLES GOUNOD

29

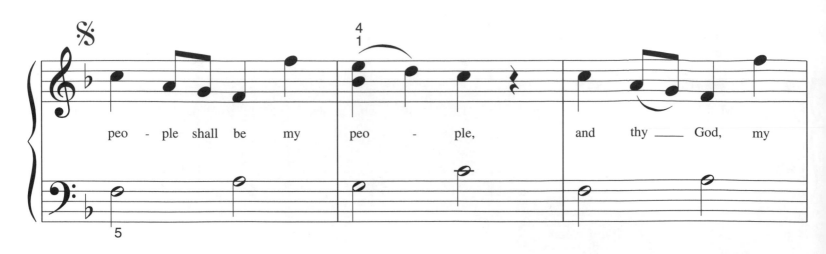

peo - ple shall be my peo - ple, and thy _____ God, my

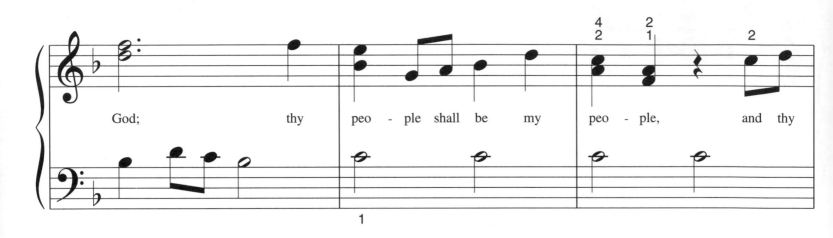

God; thy peo - ple shall be my peo - ple, and thy

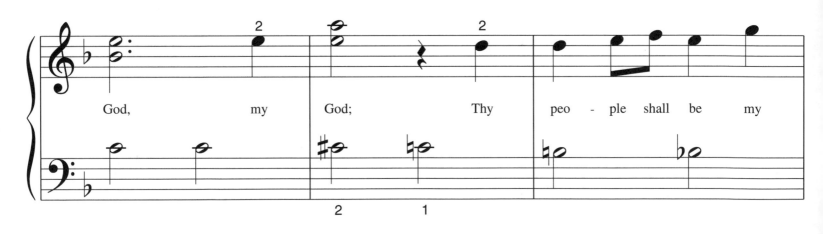

God, my God; Thy peo - ple shall be my

Fine
(last time)

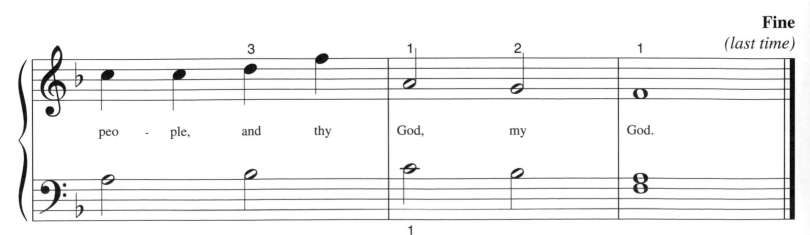

peo - ple, and thy God, my God.

JESU, JOY OF MAN'S DESIRING

By JOHANN SEBASTIAN BACH

Calmly (each measure = 1 slow beat)

LARGO
from XERXES

By GEORGE FRIDERIC HANDEL

Slowly and solemnly

MEDITATION
from THAÏS

By JULES MASSENET

Moderately slow

Agitated

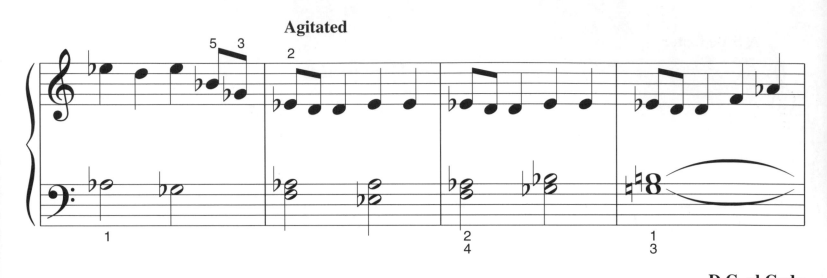

D.C. al Coda

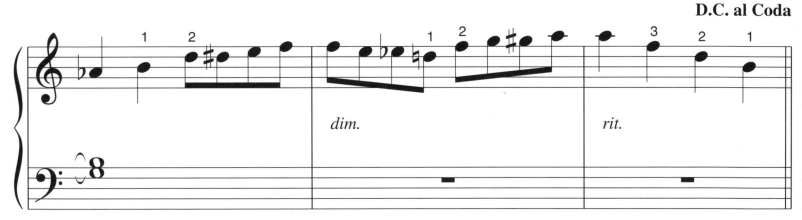

dim.

rit.

CODA

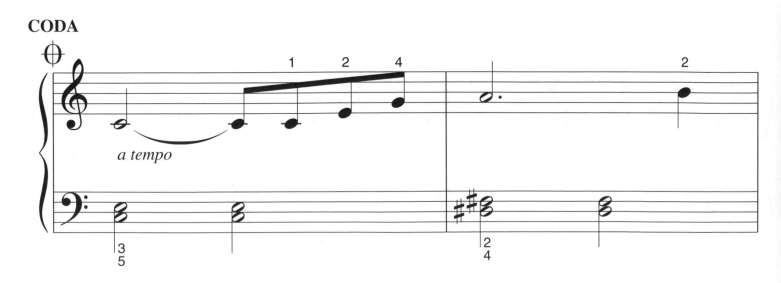

a tempo

MY HEART EVER FAITHFUL
from CANTATA 68

By JOHANN SEBASTIAN BACH

Moderately, with motion

HORNPIPE
from WATER MUSIC

By GEORGE FRIDERIC HANDEL

With energy

NIMROD
from ENIGMA VARIATIONS

By EDWARD ELGAR

Slowly

ODE TO JOY
from SYMPHONY NO. 9 in D Minor
Fourth Movement Choral Theme

Words by HENRY VAN DYKE
Music by LUDWIG VAN BEETHOVEN

PANIS ANGELICUS
(O Lord Most Holy)

By CÉSAR FRANCK

56

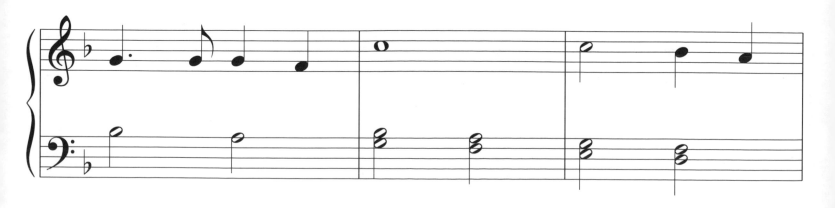

RONDEAU

By JEAN-JOSEPH MOURET

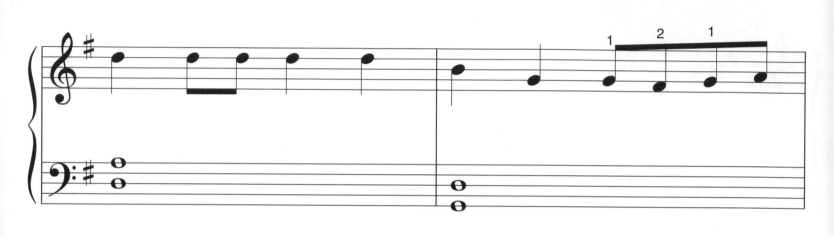

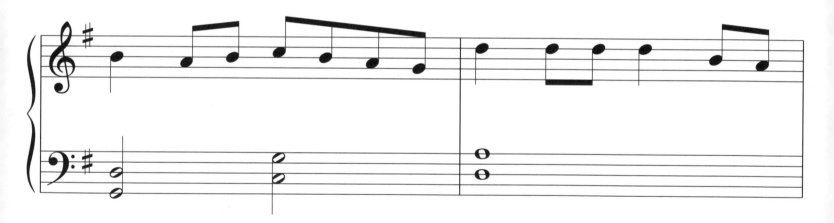

SHEEP MAY SAFELY GRAZE
from CANTATA 208

By JOHANN SEBASTIAN BACH

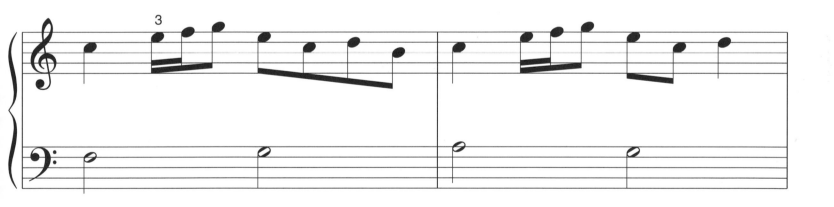

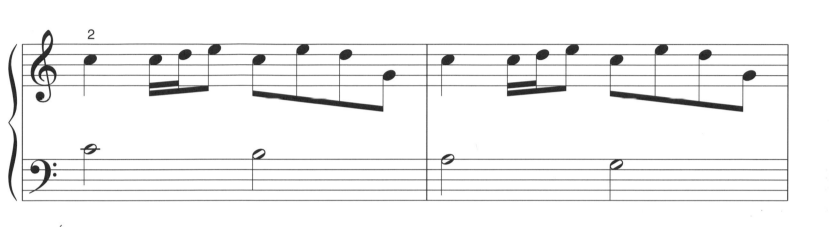

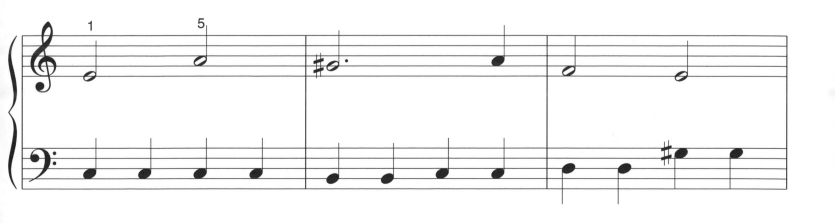

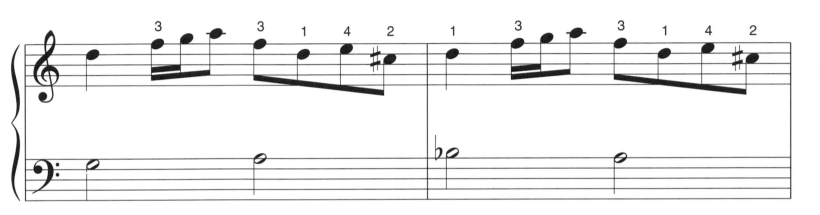

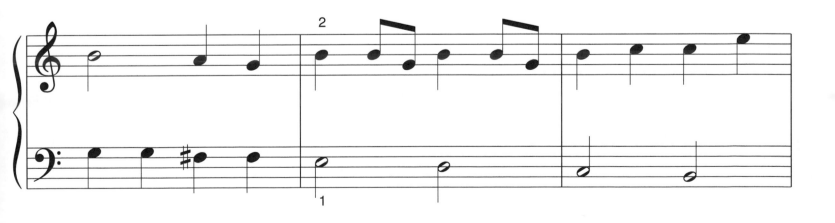

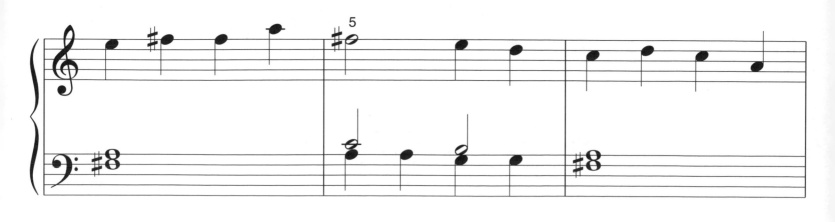

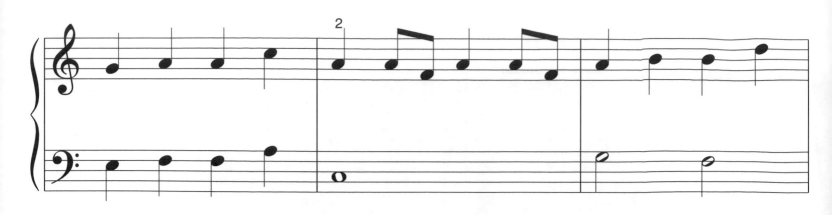

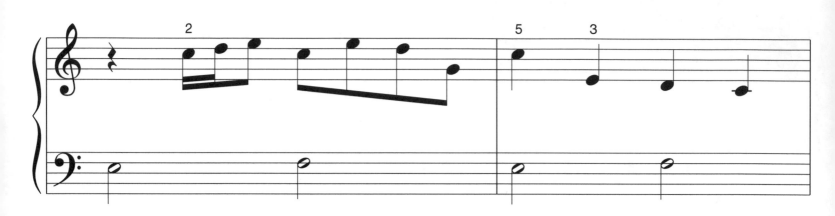

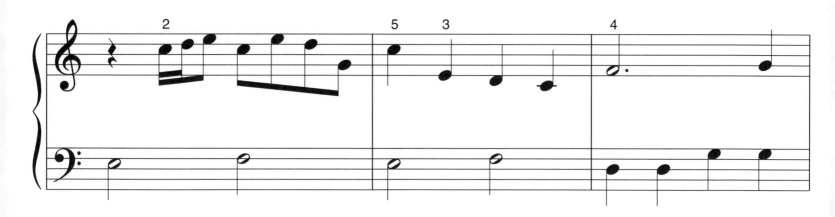

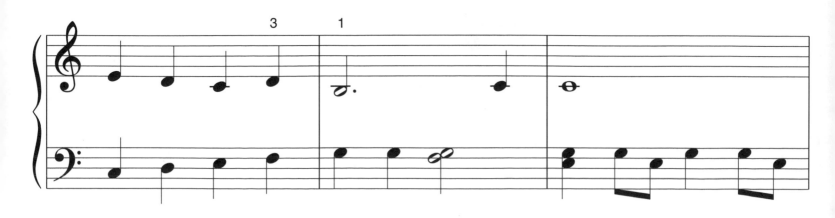

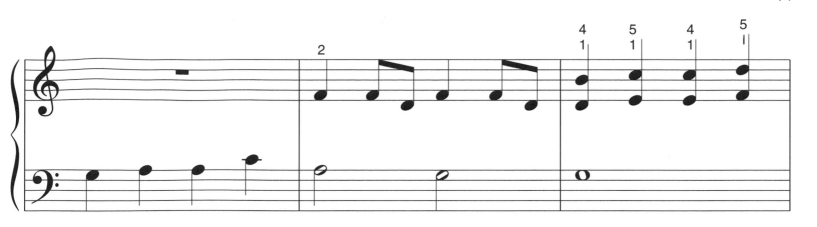

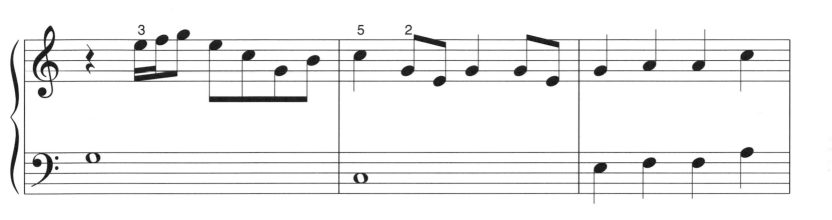

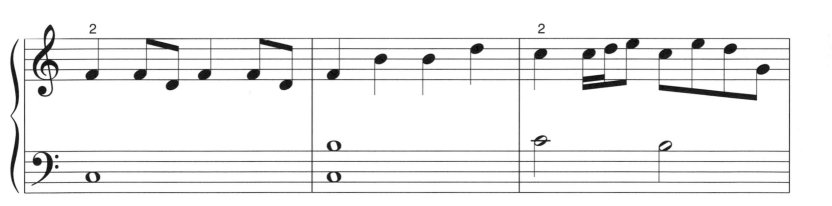

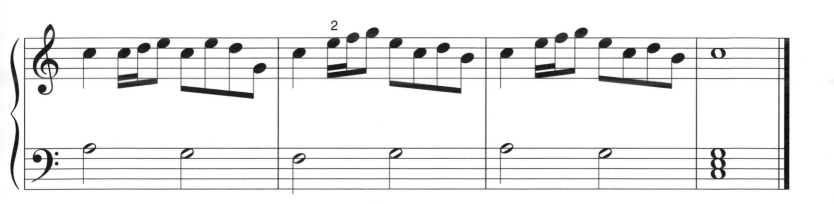

TRUMPET TUNE

By HENRY PURCELL

Stately

TRUMPET VOLUNTARY

By JEREMIAH CLARKE

Moderately, with motion

WEDDING MARCH
from A MIDSUMMER NIGHT'S DREAM

By FELIX MENDELSSOHN

Moderately fast

BIG FUN WITH BIG-NOTE PIANO BOOKS!
These songbooks feature exciting easy arrangements for beginning piano students.

Broadway Classics
Bill Boyd
12 broadway favorites for big note piano, including: Don't Cry for Me Argentina • Give My Regards to Broadway • If I Were a Rich Man • Memory • The Sound of Music • and more.
00290180 ....$7.95

Broadway Favorites
Bill Boyd
12 Broadway favorites for big-note piano, including: All I Ask of You • Edelweiss • Everything's Coming Up Roses • I Dreamed a Dream • Sunrise, Sunset • and more!
00290184 ....$7.95

Children's Favorites
14 songs children love, including: The Brady Bunch • Casper the Friendly Ghost • Going to the Zoo • The Grouch Song • Hakuna Matata • The Name Game • The Siamese Cat Song • Winnie the Pooh • more.
00310282 ....$7.95

A Christmas Collection
33 simplified favorites, including: The Christmas Song (Chestnuts Roasting) • Frosty the Snow Man • A Holly Jolly Christmas • I Saw Mommy Kissing Santa Claus • Mister Santa • The Most Wonderful Day of the Year • Nuttin' for Christmas • Silver Bells • and more.
00221818 ....$10.95

Classical Music's Greatest Hits
24 beloved classical pieces including: Air on the G String • Ave Maria • By the Beautiful Blue Danube • Canon in D • Eine Kleine Nachtmusik • Für Elise • Ode to Joy • Romeo and Juliet • Waltz of the Flowers • more.
00310475...$9.95

Country Favorites
28 songs, including: Achy Breaky Heart • Down at the Twist & Shout • God Bless the U.S.A. • Your Cheatin' Heart • and more.
00222554 ....$10.95

Disney Movie Magic
Big-note arrangements of 12 Disney movie songs: Arabian Nights • Beauty and the Beast • Circle of Life • Colors of the Wind • God Help the Outcasts • Hakuna Matata • Kiss the Girl • Part of Your World • Someday • Something There • A Whole New World • more.
00310194...$10.95

Great Jazz Standards
arranged by Bill Boyd
20 songs, including: April in Paris • Don't Get Around Much Anymore • How High the Moon • It Don't Mean a Thing (If It Ain't Got That Swing) • When I Fall in Love • and more.
00222575 ....$12.95

Hymn Favorites
Includes 20 favorite hymns: Abide with Me • Blest Be the Tie That Binds • Jesus Loves Me • Nearer My God to Thee • Rock of Ages • What a Friend We Have in Jesus • and more.
00221802 ....$6.95

Les Misérables
14 songs, including: At the End of the Day • Bring Him Home • Castle On a Cloud • Do You Hear the People Sing • I Dreamed a Dream • In My Life • On My Own • and more.
00221812 ....$12.95

Disney's Tarzan
8 great Phil Collins tunes from the animated Disney hit: Son of Man • Strangers like Me • Trashin' the Camp • Two Worlds • Two Worlds (Finale) • Two Worlds (Reprise) • You'll Be in My Heart • You'll Be in My Heart (Pop Version).
00316049 ....$12.95

Movie Hits
21 songs popularized on the silver screen, including: Beauty and the Beast • Don't Worry Be Happy • Endless Love • The Rainbow Connection • Somewhere Out There • Tears in Heaven • Unchained Melody • Under the Sea • A Whole New World • and more.
00221804 ....$9.95

Patriotic Gems
arr. Bill Boyd
20 American classics, including: America • America, The Beautiful • Battle Hymn of the Republic • Semper Fidelis • Star Spangled Banner • You're a Grand Old Flag • and more.
00221801 ....$6.95

TV Hits
Over 20 theme songs that everyone knows, including: Brady Bunch • Cheers • (Meet) The Flintstones • Home Improvement • The Jetsons • Northern Exposure • Mr. Ed • The Munsters Theme • Won't You Be My Neighbor • and more fun favorites!
00221805 ....$9.95

Prices, contents, and availability subject to change without notice.
Disney artwork © Disney Enterprises, Inc.

FOR MORE INFORMATION, SEE YOUR LOCAL MUSIC DEALER,
OR WRITE TO:

HAL•LEONARD®
CORPORATION
7777 W. BLUEMOUND RD. P.O. BOX 13819 MILWAUKEE, WI 53213
www.halleonard.com

0100